Terror and Discord

The Freeman's Journal

FIRST ESTABLISHED 1763.

DUBLIN: JULY 1, 1922.

The Shemus Cartoons in the *Freeman's Journal*, 1920–1924

THE FREEMAN'S JOURNAL, THURSDAY, AUGUST 24, 1922. 5

HOW GENERAL COLLINS DIED LEADING HIS MEN

A HERO TO THE END

COMMANDER-IN-CHIEF'S BRAVERY UNDER DEADLY FIRE

SLAIN BY PARTING VOLLEY

"FORGIVE THEM": LEADER'S LAST WORDS AS HE PASSES AWAY

General Michael Collins met his death like a soldier and a hero, leading his men to victory.

With some brother officers of the General Staff, he had been on a tour of inspection of National posts in West Cork.

Owing to road obstructions, the direct road back to the city was not available, and the military party—comprising the Generals, an armoured car and about 20 soldiers—made a detour which brought them near Crookstown, between Macroom and Bandon. It was then 6.30 o'clock on Tuesday evening.

At Bealnablath, close to Crookstown, heavy fire was opened on the troops, the first bullets nearly striking General Collins. Coolly the Chief took charge of operations, amid a hail of lead, and for close on an hour the battle raged steadily. During the fight large numbers of Irregulars were killed or wounded.

It was a parting volley, discharged when the attackers were in retreat that claimed General Collins for a victim. Though mortally wounded in the head, he fought on until he collapsed.

Before he passed away in the arms of his colleagues on that bleak roadside, he uttered these last noble words—"Forgive them."

The only other casualty on the side of the National forces was a wounded despatch rider.

MANY AMBUSHERS KILLED IN FIGHT

(From Our Special Representative.)

Cork, Wednesday Night.

General Collins was one of a party of distinguished military chiefs who left Cork City at 6 a.m. on Tuesday morning on a tour of inspection throughout county Cork. The party included Major-General Dalton, and they visited many southern posts occupied by the National Army.

THE OFFICIAL ACCOUNT

The following official bulletin was issued from Army Headquarters yesterday:—

"General Michael Collins, Commander-in-Chief of the Army, was killed in an ambush by Irregulars at Bealnablath, between Macroom and Bandon ..."

THE FATAL DETOUR

GENERAL TAKES CHARGE

AGAINST FEARFUL ODDS

MORTALLY WOUNDED

"FORGIVE THEM"

A HERO TO THE END

Chief Inspires Colleagues With His Courage

QUICKLY RALLIED

HE FOUGHT ON

THE PARTING MESSAGE

IRELAND'S VIA DOLOROSA.

WORLD SYMPATHY

Throughout Ireland and all over the world the news of the death of General Collins has caused a profound sensation. Sorrow is the predominant note, and the general sentiment is expressed in dozens of messages of sympathy, some of which we reproduce on page 6.

THE NEWS ABROAD

Deep Sorrow In America And Australia

WORLD-FAMED FIGURE

INSPIRATION TO YOUTH

AUSTRALIA MOVED

A FRENCH HOPE

HE CANNOT DIE

"Michael Collins Will Live In The Rule Of The People"

The Publicity Department issued the following on behalf of the Government yesterday:—

A Mhuintir na hEireann.

Tá an fear ba mhó agus ba chalma in Eirinn tógtha uainn díreach nuair a bhí an buadh ag gealla trí na scamaill ar aiseirghe an Náisiún ar ar bhronn sé siúd comhachta uile a fheardachta mhórdha.

Do thárnigh chun an chine, ó cháilíocht agus mhisneach Mhíchíl Uí Choileáin, neart agus beodhacht a thug chun críche an síor-troid i gcoinnibh an Namhad Eachtrannaigh—an chríoch chaithréimeach san a bhí 'na aisling nách mór tamall ó shoin. Do scuab na tréithe céadna rómpa an cheannairc cois baile a dhin irracht ar thoradh no buadha san do scioba ó nbhúr láimh .i. an t-údarás neaspleadhach atá anois agaibh sa tír.

I ngach féith den lúth a múscladh sa Náisiún, pe'ca féith fhoirgníomhach, riarthach, údarásach no armthach a bhí ann, bhí pearsantacht Mhíchíl Uí Choileáin go soiléir agus go brostuitheach.

Do marbhuíodh é—nidh is brón agus cailliúint thar mheon dúinne. Act ní bhfagha sé bás. Mairfe sé sa rialú san na ndaoine gur thug sé a mhór-dhícheall á bhaint amach, agus gabhann a chó-oibritheoirí mar dhualgas solamanta ortha féin an rialú san do choimeád fé réim.

"WHEN VICTORY SMILED"

(TRANSLATION.)

People of Ireland,

The greatest and bravest of our countrymen has been snatched from us at the moment when victory smiled through the clouds upon the uprising of the Nation to which he had dedicated all the powers of his magnificent manhood.

The genius and courage of Michael Collins lent a force and an inspiration to the race which brought the long fight against the external enemy to the triumphant end which had become almost a dream, and swept before it the domestic revolt which tried to pluck from your hands the fruits of that triumph—your unchallenged authority in the land.

In every phase of the awakened activity of the Nation—constructive, administrative, executive, military—the personality of Michael Collins was vivid and impelling.

He has been slain to our unutterable grief and loss, but he cannot die. He will live in the rule of the people which he gave his great best to assert and confirm, and which his colleagues undertake as a solemn charge to maintain.

DIED LIKE A COLLINS

Dead Leader's Brother Hears News In Chicago

EARLY DAYS

Born In West Cork Just Thirty Years Ago

THE POPE'S SORROW

Pope Pius has been deeply moved by the news of the shooting of General Collins. This and similar incidents of recent occurrence, His Holiness said, show the need of the masses to return to the teachings of the Christian doctrine of love and peace among men, and the necessity for them to realise that violence does not secure the triumph of any cause.

AS A PUBLIC SPEAKER

Many Exciting Experiences In Brief Career.

ANSWERING INTERRUPTIONS

ALWAYS HELD HIS GROUND

NEW ARMY CHIEF

General Richard Mulcahy has been appointed Commander-in-Chief of the Army in succession to General Michael Collins.

SISTER LEAVES LONDON

GEN. DALTON UNHURT

ARRIVAL OF THE REMAINS

BARED CROWDS AWAIT FUNERAL SHIP ON DUBLIN QUAYS

EARLY MORNING SCENES

MELANCHOLY PROCESSION WENDS ITS WAY THROUGH STREETS OF SILENCE

The funeral ship bearing the remains of General Michael Collins arrived in the Liffey early this morning.

Silent crowds lined the quays. Cabinet Ministers, officers of high rank, officials, soldiers and ordinary citizens formed the waiting throng.

It was a scene to dwell in the memory.

The casket containing all that was mortal of the dead Chief was borne ashore on the shoulders of army officers, and the solemn procession proceeded on its way through the lonely streets.

The remains were conveyed to the Mortuary Chapel in St. Vincent's Hospital, where they will be until 7 o'clock this evening, when they will be removed to the City Hall. Here they will lie in state until Sunday evening, when they will be removed to the Pro-Cathedral, from where the funeral will take place for Glasnevin on Monday morning after Requiem Mass at 11 o'clock.

A SPECTACLE TO DWELL IN THE MEMORY

With due solemnity, with befitting pomp, the body of Michael Collins passed through the silent streets of Dublin early this morning. Over the cobbled quays the gun carriage, carrying the flag-draped coffin, made its way. But if those steel-clad wheels clashed against the rough pavement, the sound was drowned by the feet of the multitude who, with heads bared and bowed, marched behind. And despite the lateness of the hour, and the uncertainty of the time of arrival, ...

THE LAST POST

ECHOES OF RIFLE FIRE

PRESENT ON QUAYSIDE

THE FUNERAL

MASSES FOR THE CHIEF

MOVING SPECTACLE

SAD CORK SPECTACLE

Mourners Line Streets From Hospital To Quayside

Page 5 of the *Freeman's Journal* of 24 August 1922, then the main news page, reporting the death of Michael Collins and showing the 'Via Dolorosa' cartoon in place (see pages 46–7 below).

Terror and Discord

The Shemus Cartoons in the *Freeman's Journal*, 1920–1924

Felix M. Larkin

A. & A. Farmar
in association with the
National Library of Ireland

British Library Cataloguing in Publication Data
A CIP catalogue record for this book is available
from the British Library

ISBN 978-1-906353-17-9

First published in 2009
by
A. & A. Farmar Ltd
78 Ranelagh Village, Dublin 6, Ireland
Tel +353-1-496 3625 e-mail afarmar@iol.ie
website www.aafarmar.ie

Text designed and set by A. & A. Farmar
Printed and bound by GraphyCems

To
L. Perry Curtis Jr

Contents

List of figures and publication dates in the *Freeman's Journal*

Acknowledgements

This book is dedicated to L. Perry Curtis Jr, Professor Emeritus of History at Brown University, Providence, Rhode Island, and a pioneer in cartoon studies—his *Apes and Angels: the Irishman in Victorian Caricature*, first published in 1971, is a classic. I am grateful to him for his friendship and encouragement, and for his perceptive and helpful comments on early drafts of my introduction.

The cartoons reproduced here are published courtesy of the National Library of Ireland.

Without the support and co-operation of the staff of the National Library of Ireland, particularly those in its Prints and Drawings Department, this book would simply not have been possible. I thank especially Honora Faul, the Prints and Drawings Librarian, and her colleague Dave Phelan for their expert work in arranging the Shemus archive and making it accessible. Their work greatly facilitated my research. My thanks go also to Honora's predecessor, Joanna Finegan, who recognised the value of the archive when it came on the market in 2006 and was responsible for purchasing it for the Library. Joanna gave me lots of good advice and other invaluable assistance. Others in the Library who have helped me include Colette O'Flaherty, Sandra McDermott, Justin Furlong and Noel Stapleton.

In addition, I want to acknowledge the contributions of Ian d'Alton, Professor Norma Dawson (Queen's University, Belfast), William Gallagher (Royal Irish Academy), Philip Hamell, Stawell Heard, Stacey Herbert, Peter Lacy, Robert Marshall, Professor Robert Schmuhl (University of Notre Dame, South Bend, Indiana), Alex Robertson (Leeds City Art Gallery) and the staff of the Local Studies Library in the Central Library, Calverley Street, Leeds.

I am grateful to Gerard Danaher SC, chairman of the board of the National Library of Ireland, for his insightful Foreword. His ready acceptance of my invitation to provide the Foreword is a mark of his commitment to the Library and its community of readers and staff.

My publishers, Anna and Tony Farmar, have lavished much care and attention on this book, and I greatly appreciate their efforts.

Finally, I wish to remember two people who are no longer with us. The first is Mrs

Kathleen Bowles, a daughter of Martin Fitzgerald, the last owner of the *Freeman's Journal*. If she had not told me in 1972 who Shemus was, it would probably not have been possible for me to track him down. The other is Dr Leon Ó Broin with whom I had a conversation about the Shemus cartoons in 1973 in the most unusual circumstances. I was being interviewed for a job in the Irish civil service, and Dr Ó Broin was the chairman of my interview board. We discussed the cartoons at some length during the interview. Suffice it to say that I got the job!

Felix M. Larkin
Dublin, November 2009

Foreword

It is ironic that the Yorkshire-born 'Shemus' who, as Felix Larkin points out, contributed in part at least to the demonization of Erskine Childers could well have attracted from opponents of the Treaty the same appellation of 'damned Englishman' that Arthur Griffith so famously and effectively attached to Childers.

This is only the most obvious of the many little known but fascinating historical details that make Mr Larkin's introduction to this book and his notes on the reproduced cartoons so stimulating.

However, it is the cartoons themselves which are the stars of this production although it has to be said that, without the excellent explanatory notes provided by Mr Larkin, many of the cartoons with multiple caricatures would not be remotely as intelligible to readers today as they were to contemporary readers of the *Freeman's Journal*.

In this regard, the familiarity which clearly Shemus could assume the average reader of the *Freeman's Journal* would have with so many of the Westminster cabinet is in itself an interesting reflection of the sea change in the popular political focus which followed on independence.

The prominence afforded the Shemus cartoons and the frequency of their publication in the *Freeman's Journal*, which was then still a major national daily, clearly demonstrates their popularity and influence with the paper's readers. If they had not been popular, then regardless of the talent of Shemus as a cartoonist—and indeed as an artist—commercial considerations would surely have intervened.

Apart from the obvious service Mr Larkin has rendered everyone interested in the political history of the period, he has also produced a work which contributes greatly to our understanding of the evolution of cartooning in the context of popular journalism.

The cartoons certainly reflect a very different style to the vogue today. Many of them were accompanied by an amount of text which would alienate modern readers of even the broadsheets of today, and the degree of detail in the cartoons themselves is not a feature of such work today.

Indeed, while Mr Larkin is undoubtedly correct in his assertion that the cartoons 'were remarkably daring and hard-hitting' for their time, Shemus achieved his objective by the political content of his message rather than by any viciousness in his caricatural style. He undoubtedly relied, as Mr Larkin says, on often 'exaggerating an unflattering characteristic of an individual . . . [e.g.] Sir James Craig's bulk'—but, by today's standards, these exaggerations appear amusing but essentially benign. Nevertheless, his political stiletto was no less sharp than that of his present day successors. Giving legitimate political offence does not necessitate being personally offensive, contrary to what some of today's practitioners would seem to believe.

The acquisition of the Shemus cartoons by the National Library constituted a significant addition to our Prints and Drawings collection. This collection contains some of the most fascinating material possessed by the Library. I am confident that Mr Larkin's splendid book will bring not only the Shemus cartoons but also the collection of which it forms part to greater public notice.

We are all greatly indebted to Mr Larkin for making this possible and for his admirably succinct presentation of the oeuvre of such an interesting, albeit hitherto largely forgotten, contributor to Irish independence and the establishment of the State.

Gerard Danaher SC
Chairman
National Library of Ireland
Dublin, April 2009

Introduction: The Shemus cartoons

. . . A line will take us hours maybe;
Yet if it does not seem a moment's thought,
Our stitching and unstitching has been naught.
W. B. Yeats, 'Adam's Curse'

Newspaper cartoons very effectively convey political opinion, especially disapproval of policies and individuals. A good example is the series of cartoons by 'Shemus' that appeared in the *Freeman's Journal* in the early 1920s—the final years of that old and distinguished Irish newspaper. The *Freeman* published some three hundred Shemus cartoons between 1920 and 1924. It was a period of great political and military upheaval in Ireland, and the cartoons were remarkably daring and hard-hitting. Indeed, in 1923 they were described by Cathal O'Shannon, a Labour Party member of Dáil Éireann, as 'artistic bombs'.[1] Up to the Truce of July 1921 which led on to the Anglo-Irish Treaty the following December, their main target was what Roy Foster has called 'the increasingly desperate and draconian nature of British rule' in Ireland at that time.[2] Thereafter they attacked the new government of Northern Ireland and the anti-Treaty elements in the new Irish Free State with all the venom previously directed against the British authorities. They thus reflected, and reinforced, the editorial policy of the *Freeman*. Moreover, the *Freeman*'s sense that it was itself an important player in the unfolding drama was evident in the cartoons. During the War of Independence, for instance, the *Freeman* saw itself as a bulwark against the British government and the excesses of the British military forces in Ireland, and this underlay many Shemus cartoons—including one reproduced here (fig. 12).

Shemus was an English artist, Ernest Forbes (1879–1962), afterwards well known in London and in his native Yorkshire for his landscapes and portraits, both drawings and oil paintings.[3] He used a number of pseudonyms in his long career, and even 'Ernest Forbes' was a contrivance: his full name was Ernest Forbes Holgate and he dropped the surname when signing his work, though some of his earliest work—dating from before he came to Ireland—was signed Ernest Holgate. Various sources give his year of birth as 1877, but actually he was born in Leeds on 2 July 1879.[4] His father was Thomas Pullen Holgate, a stonemason and sculptor. Forbes was his mother's maiden name. He is recorded in the 1901 Census as living with his widowed mother in the family home in Leeds, aged 21, and working as a clerk in a newspaper office—presumably the office of the *Yorkshire Evening News*, where he honed his skills as a cartoonist. He contributed cartoons to the *News* as 'The Hermit' for many years before the First World War. He enlisted on the outbreak of war and, after a period of training, served on the western front as an artillery lieutenant. He was badly gassed in 1918 and temporarily blinded, necessitating a long period of recuperation.[5]

So why was he in Ireland during the War of Independence and its aftermath? The most likely explanation is that he was seeking a fresh start outside England following the failure of his marriage. He had married early in 1919, and the marriage lasted only a short time. His wife was a daughter of James Marshall, the wealthy owner of the Huntingdon Brewery and a grandson of the founder of Marshall & Snelgrove, the famous department store in Oxford Street, London.[6] At the time of his marriage, Forbes had a studio in Chelsea—at the very heart of London's fine art world—and was clearly attempting to establish himself as a bona fide artist.[7] Many years would pass before he realised that ambition, though he did eventually do so. In the meantime, his work as a cartoonist was a way of supporting himself—but it was always a diversion from the main purpose of his life.

As a young man in Leeds before the First World War, he had been encouraged in his artistic ambitions by Edmund Bogg, a noted writer of books about the Yorkshire Dales and other places in the north of England. Bogg gathered around himself a coterie of young artists who met regularly to draw or paint and to discuss art and from whom he commissioned illustrations for his books. Forbes was a member of this set. In the words of W. R. Mitchell, writing about Forbes in the *Dalesman* magazine, 'art ruled his life'.[8] A journalist colleague on the *Freeman*, James Winder Good, likewise wrote of him that 'good painting is with Mr Forbes a passion'.[9] He exhibited in the Royal Hibernian Academy during his years in Ireland,[10] and had at least one solo exhibition of landscapes and other paintings in Dublin—held in a prestigious city centre gallery in September 1922.[11] He later participated in exhibitions of the Royal Portrait Society and the Royal Academy in London. A member of the Royal Society of British Artists from 1926, he had a solo exhibition in London in 1936 entitled 'Humour in Art', which was reviewed in *The Times*.[12]

The Shemus cartoons began to appear in the *Freeman's Journal* at the end of January 1920, but did not become a regular feature until the following June. From then until June

1921, an average of about nine were published each month. After that, their frequency varied greatly and in some months none or very few were published. In fact, over two-thirds of the post-June 1921 cartoons fall into three distinct periods—November–December 1921, April–November 1922 and July–October 1923—which together represent less than half the time that elapsed before the *Freeman* went out of business. The layout of the *Freeman* varied from day to day, and a page could comprise either seven or eight columns of news and other items. The cartoons were usually three columns wide and close to square in shape, and were placed in the top centre of the page opposite the editorials (see the frontispiece). When occasionally they appeared elsewhere, it was almost always on the front page. One of the previous week's cartoons would then be repeated on the front page of the *Weekly Freeman*.

Except for the the first six, the cartoons were generally signed with a distinctive monogram—the cartoonist's pen name written with some distortion of its letters so as to suggest a circle. Each cartoon was given a title and, normally, a caption consisting of two or more lines of text. The text, while sometimes a little stilted, is nevertheless often the means by which the cartoon packs its punch. The cartoons rely heavily on caricature for their effect, but also important is the placing of individuals in comical situations which enlarge on their foibles or reveal an angle on events unflattering to them. The best of them express a sense of outrage without compromising their essential humour, and this gives them their force. The cartoons are uncluttered, characterised by bold and confident lines—the product of skilful draughtsmanship.

In December 2006 the National Library of Ireland acquired an archive of about 280 items by Ernest Forbes, mostly original drawings of Shemus cartoons.[13] Three of the Shemus cartoons, including one reproduced here (fig. 4, also the cover illustration), are in watercolour; the rest are pen-and-ink drawings in black and white, with often a little shading in blue crayon. Needless to say, they were published in the *Freeman* in black and white. The archive has the originals of over three-quarters of the Shemus cartoons published by the *Freeman*, together with about thirty more which appear never to have been published—it has not, in any event, been possible to trace them in the newspaper. The archive includes, in addition, some original caricature portraits of notable persons also signed with the Shemus monogram and original drawings of other cartoons by Forbes which he signed as 'Cormac'. The latter are in a style markedly different from the Shemus cartoons and portraits, and are usually concerned with sporting events such as horse-racing at Dublin or British venues. The portraits and the Cormac cartoons were also published in the *Freeman*, the Cormac cartoons from mid-1922 onwards and the portraits in a series entitled 'Snapped by Shemus' between February and July 1923.

When the 'Snapped by Shemus' series was running, it largely superseded the Shemus cartoons. Only a small number of cartoons were published in the first half of 1923, presumably because Forbes was fully engaged in producing the portraits instead. Seventy-four portraits were published in total, and most are of Free State politicians. The subjects, with dates of publication, are listed in the Appendix. The original drawings of just eighteen are included in the archive of Forbes' work acquired by the National Library in 2006. Happily, they have been supplemented by the purchase of a further ten, all of which carry the signature 'Ernest Forbes' as well as, with one exception, the Shemus monogram.[14] There are a few duplicates between the two acquisitions, but the Library now has original portraits of twenty-four of the subjects in the 'Snapped by Shemus' series.[15] The *Freeman* also published at various times five portraits by Shemus which were not part of the series, but the Library holds no originals of these.[16]

The illustrations of cartoons and portraits in this book are taken from the original drawings in the Library's collection. I have tried to pick a selection that fairly represents the work that Forbes did for the *Freeman*, while favouring cartoons that relate to significant events or strike me as of outstanding quality. The items chosen are grouped thematically: the War of Independence; the Truce and the Anglo-Irish Treaty of 1921; the Civil War; the *Freeman*'s self-image; caricature portraits; Northern Ireland; and independent Ireland. In presenting the cartoons, I have used the titles and captions that were actually published in the *Freeman*—not always the same as Forbes' draft titles and captions, though the differences between the two are generally insignificant. Where they are significant, I have recorded Forbes' alternative suggestions—sometimes, though not always, superior to what was printed.

When Forbes joined the *Freeman's Journal* in 1920, the paper's principal proprietor was Martin Fitzgerald—a rambunctious figure, who had founded a well-known firm of wine merchants in Dublin and was prominent in the commercial and sporting life of the city in the early years of the last century.[17] His main sporting interest was in horse-racing. An associate of his in horse-racing circles was R. Hamilton Edwards, a retired British journalist who had once worked with Lord Northcliffe in London but was now living in Ireland. Fitzgerald and Edwards jointly purchased the *Freeman's Journal* in October 1919. It had been the semi-official organ of the Irish Party at Westminster since Parnell's time. Accordingly, after the 1918 General Election and Sinn Féin's triumph over that nationalist tradition, it lost its *raison d'être* and was forced into liquidation some weeks before its purchase by Fitzgerald and Edwards. It is likely that Hamilton Edwards, with his experience and connections in London, recruited Forbes to the *Freeman*—and the Shemus cartoons are broadly similar in style to cartoons that had been appearing in London newspapers such as the *Daily Mirror* and the *Daily Mail*, both Northcliffe publications. The work of W. K. Haselden in the former and Percy Fearon (known as 'Poy') in the latter would have been familiar to Edwards, and probably to Forbes too: both were near contemporaries of Forbes. As a caricaturist, Forbes bears comparison with another near contemporary in London journalism, the great Max Beerbohm.[18]

Forbes remained essentially a British cartoonist in exile throughout his sojourn in Ireland, at his best when treating of his Irish subject matter from the perspective of British politics and focusing on British politicians. His pseudonym 'Shemus'—an unmistakably English rendition of the Irish name 'Séamus'—was, therefore, entirely appropriate.[19] Moreover, his cartoons in the *Freeman* during the War of Independence mirrored the British liberal critique of British policy in Ireland—a critique based principally on what British journalists were reporting from Ireland.[20] Lloyd George features prominently in these cartoons, and the London *Times* later said of them that 'Shemus sharpens his wits over Mr Lloyd George more cleverly and variously than many of his colleagues. We see the Prime Minister puzzled, angry, nervous—not always that smiling imp of mischief which some of our caricaturists too persistently make him.'[21] When the British presence in Ireland wound down in 1922 and Forbes was deprived of a British context for his work, his Shemus cartoons became much less subtle and insightful—and eventually he produced fewer of them.

There was a rich heritage of newspaper cartoons in Ireland. In the late 19th century, the wonderfully vivid and colourful cartoons published by the *Freeman* and other organs of nationalist opinion in Dublin were immensely popular—and they are still often reproduced. These cartoons were distributed gratis as supplements by the *Weekly Freeman* from the 1870s, and copied by others—notably *United Ireland*, the weekly newspaper founded by Parnell in 1881 and edited by William O'Brien. Curiously, there was no equivalent in the British press.[22] They were very different from the Shemus cartoons—less humorous and more propagandistic, sometimes little more than visual representations of news stories. They had been discontinued for some time before Forbes came to work for the *Freeman*, and it is unlikely that he was aware of them. The only possible echo of them in his work is the occasional depiction of the iconic female figure of Erin—notably, in a series of cartoons about the peace conference in Dublin in April 1922 which tried unsuccessfully to halt the drift to civil war, the first of which is reproduced as fig. 8.[23] Even that echo is doubtful since the use of a beautiful female figure to represent Ireland was common also in British cartoons in the late 19th century—and, in any event, it had a much older lineage both in Ireland and England.[24]

It would be wrong, however, to view the Shemus cartoons simply as the work of Ernest Forbes. They cannot be divorced from the newspaper in which they appeared—the *Freeman's Journal*. Under its new proprietors, Fitzgerald and Edwards, the *Freeman* retained the moderate nationalist sympathies that had long been its editorial hallmark and it continued to uphold the broadly liberal values of the defunct Home Rule movement. It advocated Dominion status for Ireland during the War of Independence and then strongly supported the Anglo-Irish Treaty of 1921. It was fearless in opposing the excesses of the British military forces in Ireland during the War of Independence and later in opposing those who rejected the Treaty. The difficulties it encountered were extraordinary. The British authorities suppressed it for seven weeks from December 1919 to January 1920. Fitzgerald, Edwards and the editor, Patrick J. Hooper, were imprisoned in Mountjoy Jail for a month at Christmas 1920 after the *Freeman* published a story of army brutality. Its printing presses were smashed by an armed raiding party of anti-Treatyites in March 1922 because of its stance against the anti-Treaty forces, and in December 1922 Fitzgerald was ordered to quit Ireland on pain of death by the anti-Treaty forces. He published a facsimile of that threat in the *Freeman*, but otherwise ignored it.[25] Forbes' initial cartoon for the *Freeman* was in the first edition of the newspaper published after its suppression in December 1919 and January 1920.[26]

Martin Fitzgerald played a key part in the process leading up to the 1921 Treaty. Once the British government decided to explore settlement possibilities in Ireland, he was able—and willing—to use his standing as a newspaper proprietor to act as an intermediary between Sinn Féin and Dublin Castle. He was in regular contact with both Michael Collins and Alfred ('Andy') Cope, the shadowy assistant under-secretary at the Castle who conducted most of the secret British negotiations with the Irish leaders in the period before the Truce. Fitzgerald's role as a go-between is well attested in contemporary documents.[27] His relationship with Cope took on a further aspect when, during the Treaty negotiations, the latter set about rallying support in Ireland for the emerging settlement. Through Fitzgerald, Cope gained a measure of influence over the contents of the *Freeman's Journal* at that time—reflecting the fact that both wished to secure acceptance of the settlement on offer. The *Freeman*'s subsequent campaign in favour of the Treaty was generally regarded, even on the pro-Treaty side, as unduly partisan. It was marked by intemperate editorials, the suppression of anti-Treaty manifestos and speeches, and a notably malevolent treatment of Erskine Childers that included a Shemus cartoon depicting de Valera as the mouthpiece of Childers which appeared on 10 February 1922 (fig. 7).

Desmond Ryan, who was also on the *Freeman*'s staff in the 1920s, recalls in his memoir *Remembering Sion* that the Childers cartoon so disgusted him that he resolved to leave the *Freeman* on account of it.[28] He says that Martin Fitzgerald himself 'ordered his cartoonist to draw [that] very bitter cartoon'.[29] This comment from an insider demonstrates the constraints within which Forbes produced his work for the *Freeman*. These constraints are not really surprising: the Shemus cartoons were subject to the editorial policy of the newspaper, not independent of it—and editorial policy was, in turn, subject to proprietorial diktat. There is further evidence of the subordination of the cartoons to editorial policy in a query to a sub-editor scribbled by Forbes at the bottom of the original drawing of his cartoon 'Ulster will fight' (fig. 24). It reads: 'Would you please ask Mr Donovan to confirm the letterpress of this cartoon. He telephoned the idea and I doubt whether the wording is right.' The published caption is exactly as proposed by Forbes. The man who gave him the idea for the cartoon was Professor Robert Donovan, then in charge of writing the editorials in the *Freeman*.[30]

Fitzgerald's interfering hand is doubtless to be seen also in the fascinating Cormac cartoon about the production of the newspaper on Gestetner machines as a stop-gap following the destruction of its printing presses in March 1922 (fig. 14). Fitzgerald gloried in defying the anti-Treatyites who had destroyed his plant in the hope of silencing him, and this shines through Forbes' cartoon. It was published on 22 April 1922 when the *Freeman* resumed normal production, and is in the same style and has the same layout as Forbes' other Cormac cartoons. A Shemus cartoon published in the *Freeman* on the same day celebrated the newspaper's re-appearance in a similarly triumphant tone (fig. 13). Likewise, given that horse-racing was Martin Fitzgerald's favourite sport, it is hardly just coincidental that a race meeting was the usual occasion of a Cormac cartoon. Moreover, twenty-five of Forbes' caricature portraits—about a third of them—are of Fitzgerald's colleagues in the Free State Senate. Fitzgerald was nominated to the Senate in December 1922, partly to represent the old Home Rule tradition but also because the new administration in Dublin had come increasingly to rely on the *Freeman*'s support in shaping public opinion.

The *Freeman*'s unquestioning support of the government prompted Cathal O'Shannon's 'artistic bombs' remark about the Shemus cartoons. O'Shannon was speaking in a debate in Dáil Éireann in 1923 against a government proposal to prescribe a sentence of flogging for some offences. The *Freeman* had strongly opposed a similar measure introduced earlier in Northern Ireland, thus inspiring several mordant Shemus cartoons emphasising the cruelty of such punishment.[31] O'Shannon commented as follows:

> I do not suppose that tomorrow morning the *Freeman's Journal* will dare to republish the cartoon which it published twelve or eighteen months ago when the Flogging Bill was brought into the Belfast Parliament. No, this is the Parliament of the Saorstát [Irish Free State] and that was the Parliament of the Six Counties [of Northern Ireland]. You can fire artistic bombs at the Parliament of the Six Counties, but do not touch the Parliament of the Saorstát.[32]

The last Shemus cartoon appeared in the *Freeman* on 15 November 1924. Its subject was Sir Edward Carson and the Northern Irish unionists, a regular butt of the Shemus cartoons. Carson was the great *bête noir* of the cartoons, and was included in more of them than anyone else. Not even Lloyd George at the height of the War of Independence had featured in them as frequently as Carson. It was, therefore, an appropriate valedictory—though, almost certainly, an unintended one. Forbes, however, could not have been surprised when just over a month later—on 19 December 1924—the *Freeman* ceased publication. Fitzgerald had lost a lot of money in attempting to revive its fortunes, and the newspaper's parlous financial condition was inevitably worsened by its tribulations during the War of Independence and afterwards. The immediate cause of its demise was that the partnership of Fitzgerald and Edwards ended in grief when the latter tried unsuccessfully to corner the market in newsprint and then absconded, leaving debts that the enfeebled *Freeman* could not meet. The *Freeman*'s assets, including the title, were later bought by the *Irish Independent*, which for many years afterwards carried in its masthead the legend 'Incorporating the *Freeman's Journal*'.[33]

Forbes returned to London, where he worked on the London *Evening News* and contributed caricatures to the *Illustrated London News*, sometimes under his old pen name 'The Hermit': one of these depicted Sir John Reith of the BBC in Roman toga, with the caption ' B.B. Caesar'! In the early 1930s, he re-established his connections with Yorkshire when he wrote a long series of pictorial articles for the *Yorkshire Post* on the cities, towns and villages of Yorkshire and the ordinary people of the county—illustrated with his own drawings. Entitled 'This Mellow Shire', it was probably his best work—for him, a labour of love. To quote his obituarist in the *Yorkshire Post*, in these articles Forbes 'proved himself as much an artist in words as with the pencil . . . His drawings were both elegant and full of sharp observation.'[34] With the success of this series, he was able to give up his work for newspapers in the late 1930s and concentrate on oil painting, particularly landscapes. He moved back to Yorkshire, settling at first in Askwith, near Otley, and then in Harrogate. Bizarrely, in 1946 he suffered severe head injuries and fractured ribs when attacked by a bull while painting in a field in Askwith. He died in February 1962, aged eighty-two. His identity was by then so completely subsumed in his artistic persona that the name on his death certificate is Ernest Forbes, not Ernest Forbes Holgate.[35]

He never remarried, and was described by W. R. Mitchell as 'solitary but not lonely'.[36] Mitchell also tells us that he was 'a tall, handsome man who, in his young days, was very athletic. He had a fairly deep voice, and expressed himself directly, with no verbal frills.'[37] 'No frills' is a phrase that could equally be applied to his Shemus cartoons. Their apparent simplicity is part of their appeal and it enabled Forbes to hit the right note again and again, making his work both immediate and memorable. James Winder Good identified this quality when reviewing Forbes' solo exhibition in Dublin in 1922 for the *Freeman*: 'Nothing is left to chance in Mr Forbes' work: what he gets, he gets by patient and calculated effort. Yet not the least merit of his pictures is that this effort is not obtruded in the finished work.'[38] Since the same can be said of the Shemus cartoons, they exemplify the very high standard of creative achievement so elegantly defined in the epigraph to this introduction.

The *Freeman* was fully aware of the asset it had in Ernest Forbes. The 'famous Shemus cartoons' featured strongly in its advertising and other publicity.[39] As early as June 1920, for example, they were the subject of an editorial in the newspaper—which, under the headline 'Our Cartoonist', observed that 'every new sketch from him means a keen commentary on the situation in Ireland, a pictorial satire, witty, humorous or biting, and always illuminating . . . and his cartoons have a high political value which we think is properly appreciated by readers of this journal'.[40] Moreover, when launching the 'Snapped by Shemus' feature—the series of his caricature portraits of notable persons published in 1923—the *Freeman* lauded him as 'this gifted artist' and proclaimed that his cartoons 'will not easily fade from public memory . . . [and] are amongst the most notable productions in the history of the cartoonist's art'.[41] That may be an extravagant boast, but the cartoons did light up the pages of the *Freeman's Journal* between 1920 and 1924. With the National Library's acquisition of such a large number of the original drawings of the cartoons, it is likely that they will again become well known—deservedly so, for they are eminently suitable for use as illustrations in academic and other studies. They are 'abstracts and brief chronicles of the time', to quote Hamlet.[42] A selection of the best of the Shemus cartoons for the years 1920 and 1921 is already available in book form, but that volume—called *The Reign of Terror*, and published by the *Freeman* itself in 1922—is now extremely rare and hard to find, even in libraries.[43] The following extract from the review of it in the London

Times will serve as an appropriate conclusion: 'Shemus is indeed quite a master of his particular genre. He is not too bitter to forget to be humorous and some of his cartoons . . . are really laughable.'[44]

1 *Dáil Debates,* vol. 3, col. 2935, 26 June 1923.
2 Roy Foster, 'The dancer and the dance: the performance of Yeats' life' in Alistair Horne (ed.), *Telling lives: from W. B. Yeats to Bruce Chatwin* (London, 2000), p. 274.
3 Most of my biographical information about Forbes has been gleaned from a lengthy obituary in the *Yorkshire Post,* 20 February 1962. See also the 'Old Yorkshire Diary' feature in the *Yorkshire Evening Post,* 18 July 1983. In addition, I have relied on two articles in the *Dalesman* magazine, both written by W. R. Mitchell: 'The life and times of Ernest Forbes: a Yorkshire artist' (October 1987) and 'Weaving magic with both prose and pencil' (September 1997).
4 Birth certificate from the General Register Office for England.
5 See *Yorkshire Evening News,* 18 March 1918.
6 Marriage certificate from the General Register Office for England. His wife was Theresa Constance Marshall, and they were married in Christ Church, Chelsea, on 14 February 1919. He was aged 39 (though he gave his age in the certificate as 38), and she was 22.
7 His address given in his marriage certificate was '7 Chelsea Manor—studios'.
8 Mitchell, 'Weaving magic with both prose and pencil'.
9 *Freeman's Journal,* 16 September 1922.
10 He had two paintings in the RHA annual exhibition in 1922, and his address was given as 13 Fitzwilliam Square (see Ann M. Stewart, *Royal Hibernian Academy of Arts: index of exhibitors and their works, 1826–1979,* 3 vols (Dublin, 1986), i, p. 268).
11 The exhibition was held in the Gallery, 10 St Stephen's Green, Dublin. James Winder Good reviewed it for the *Freeman's Journal* on 16 September 1922.
12 *The Times,* 2 June 1936. The exhibition was also noticed in *The Studio* magazine, vol. 112 (1936), p. 102. It was held at the Leger Galleries, Old Bond Street, London.
13 The National Library of Ireland reference is PD 4309 TX.
14 The National Library of Ireland reference is PD 4319 TX. The portrait of Colonel Maurice Moore (fig. 15) doesn't have the Shemus monogram.
15 Details of the duplicate holdings are as follows: there are two original portraits of Senator T. W. Westropp Bennett, two of Senator Cornelius J. Irwin and three of Ernest Blythe TD (including fig. 18).
16 The subjects and dates of publication of these caricature portraits are: Sir Hamar Greenwood, *Freeman's Journal,* 6 May 1920; Sir Edward Carson, *Freeman's Journal,* 28 May 1920; Sir Thomas Lipton, *Freeman's Journal,* 24 July 1920; T. P. O'Connor MP, *Weekly Freeman,* 18 November 1922; and John McCormack, *Freeman's Journal,* 18 January 1923.
17 For a full account of the *Freeman*'s history, see Felix M. Larkin, 'A great daily organ: the *Freeman's Journal,* 1763–1924', in *History Ireland,* 14:3 (May/June 2006), pp 44–9. I have

written the entry on Martin Fitzgerald for the Royal Irish Academy's *Dictionary of Irish Biography* (Cambridge, 2009).

18 For examples of the work of Haselden (1872–1953), Fearon (1874–1948) and Beerbohm (1872–1956), see *100 British cartoonists of the century* (London, 2000). Ernest Forbes is not included in this volume, though he should be regarded as a British cartoonist. Perhaps because of his many pseudonyms, he has received no recognition for his work as a cartoonist—until now, of course.

19 Given Forbes' nationality and his evident disdain for British policy in Ireland, his Shemus moniker could be deconstructed as meaning 'shame-on-us'. I am grateful to Professor L. P. Curtis Jr for this insight.

20 For an interesting account of what British and American journalists were reporting from Ireland at this time, see Maurice Walsh, *The news from Ireland: foreign correspondents and the Irish revolution* (London and New York, 2008).

21 Quoted in the advertisements for *The reign of terror: a series of 'Shemus' cartoons printed in the* Freeman's Journal *during 1920–1* (Dublin, [1922]) that appeared in the *Freeman's Journal* (see, for example, 6 March 1922).

22 L. Perry Curtis Jr, *Images of Erin in the age of Parnell* (Dublin, 2000), pp 14–15. See also L. M. Cullen, 'Establishing a communications system: news, post and transport' in Brian Farrell (ed.), *Communications and community in Ireland* (Dublin and Cork, 1984), p. 26.

23 Professor Curtis suggests that the representations of Erin in late Victorian cartoons fall into five categories: monumental, enchained, empowered, courting and ambiguous (see *Images of Erin*, p. 16). Examples of four of these categories can be found in the limited number of Shemus cartoons that feature the iconic female figure—the exception being 'courting'. By 1920, the time for courtship was over.

24 Curtis, *Images of Erin*, pp 11–13.

25 See *Freeman's Journal*, 9 December 1922.

26 *Freeman's Journal*, 28 January 1920.

27 See, for example, Michael Hopkinson (ed.), *The last days of Dublin Castle: the Mark Sturgis diaries* (Dublin, 1999), pp 186, 194, 197.

28 Desmond Ryan, *Remembering Sion: a chronicle of storm and quiet* (London, 1934), p. 280.

29 Ibid., p. 263.

30 Robert Donovan (1862–1934) was a leader-writer on the *Freeman's Journal* from 1891 to 1923, and in 1909 was appointed the first Professor of English Literature in University College Dublin after it became a constituent college of the new National University of Ireland.

31 For relevant cartoons, see *Freeman's Journal*, 20 March 1922, 25 May 1922, 1 June 1922 and 8 August 1922. There is also an unpublished—or possibly just untraced—cartoon in the Shemus archive in the National Library of Ireland on this theme, entitled 'The Whip Hand'.

32 *Dáil Debates*, vol. 3, col. 2935, 26 June 1923. The particular cartoon mentioned by O'Shannon is probably 'Flogging Revived', published on 20 March 1922.

33 The *Freeman* had faced strong competition from the *Independent* for over thirty years, but

especially from 1905 onwards. Launched as the pro-Parnell organ in 1891, it was purchased in 1900 by William Martin Murphy. When Murphy transformed the paper in 1905 into the modern *Irish Independent*, at half the *Freeman*'s price—a halfpenny, instead of a penny—and in a more popular format, it was an immediate success.

34 *Yorkshire Post*, 20 February 1962.

35 Death certificate from the General Register Office for England.

36 Mitchell, 'Weaving magic with both prose and pencil'.

37 Mitchell, 'The life and times of Ernest Forbes'.

38 *Freeman's Journal*, 16 September 1922. The review was signed 'J.W.G.'.

39 That phrase was used in the *Freeman's Journal* on 24 August 1920.

40 *Freeman's Journal*, 22 June 1920.

41 *Freeman's Journal*, 19 February 1923. In addition, on 13 July 1921 the *Freeman* noted an appreciation of the Shemus cartoons in *The New World*—described as a magazine 'of international scope, of Franco-American-British connection'—and quoted from it.

42 *Hamlet* (1601), act 2, sc. 2.

43 See note 21 above. The publication of *The reign of terror* was announced in the *Freeman's Journal* on 16 January 1922 and reviewed there on 24 January 1922. The title page is reproduced on p. 78 below.

44 Quoted in the advertisements for *The reign of terror* that appeared in the *Freeman's Journal* (see note 21 above).

Cartoons and Portraits: A Selection

1. 'The Listowel Debate'*

Freeman's Journal, 15 July 1920

* Shemus suggested 'The Board of Guardians' as the title of this cartoon.

FEATURING 'five unscrupulous politicians' known to be hostile to Irish nationalist aspirations, this shows Shemus' skill in caricature. The occasion of the cartoon was the blocking of a debate in the House of Commons on a police mutiny that occurred in Listowel, Co. Kerry in June 1920. Fourteen RIC constables had resigned en masse when instructed to adopt a more aggressive security policy by their divisional inspector. The *Freeman* published the story—a scoop for the newspaper—on 10 July 1920.[1] The phrase 'five unscrupulous politicians' is taken from the main editorial in the *Freeman* on 10 July 1920 on the subject of the mutiny. The five were: Sir Hamar Greenwood, Chief Secretary for Ireland; Sir Walter Long, First Lord of the Admiralty and chairman of the Cabinet Committee on the Irish Situation; Bonar Law, Lord Privy Seal and leader of the Conservative Party; F. E. Smith (known as 'Galloper' Smith, now Lord Birkenhead), Lord Chancellor; and Sir Edward Carson, leader of the Ulster unionists. Carson had served in the wartime coalition governments under both Asquith and Lloyd George, but resigned in January 1918. Bonar Law and Smith had been closely associated with Carson in the Ulster unionist resistance to Home Rule in the period 1912–14.

1 For further information about the 'Listowel mutiny', see J. Anthony Gaughan, *Memoirs of Constable Jeremiah Mee, RIC* (Dublin, 1975), pp 93–151. See also Gabriel Doherty and John Borgonovo, 'Smoking gun? RIC reprisals, Summer 1920' in *History Ireland*, 17:2 (March/April 2009), pp 36–9.

Greenwood [on left] (to Long, Bonar Law, Galloper Smith and Carson [left to right])—'Say, you guys, the House has been muzzled, but I can't gag Ireland.' Carson—'Why not?' Galloper Smith—'Now, Ned, keep quiet.' Long—'And my job doesn't seem as safe and easy as I thought it was.' Bonar Law—'Why not try saying "Yes" and "No" at the same time, Hamar?'

2. 'The Reprisals Rag'
Freeman's Journal, 2 October 1920

THIS CARTOON REFERS to a number of incidents in which the crown forces sacked towns in Ireland in reprisal for local acts of violence by the IRA. It appeared on the day that the *Freeman* reported one such incident in Tobercurry, Co. Sligo—a reprisal for an attack on a police lorry in which a young RIC officer was killed. Even before that incident, however, the *Freeman* had accused the crown forces of pursuing a formal policy of reprisals in Ireland—see, for example, the main editorial of two days earlier (30 September 1920). The cartoon depicts Sir Henry Wilson (at the piano), Chief of the Imperial General Staff in London, and General Sir Neville Macready—who commanded the army in Ireland—with Sir Hamar Greenwood in the background. Its clear message is that responsibility for the indiscipline and excesses of the military in Ireland lies with their superiors at the very highest level. The caption draws a parallel with similar excesses on the part of the military after the rebellion of 1798.[1]

1 See Gabriel Doherty and John Borgonovo, 'Smoking gun? RIC reprisals, Summer 1920' in *History Ireland*, 17:2 (March/April 2009), pp 36–9

Macready [right, with fiddle]—'What will we give as an encore, Henry?'
Wilson [at the piano]—'A ballad, I think, "Ninety-eight is here again" or "The worst is yet to come".'

3. 'The Liberator'
Freeman's Journal, 26 October 1920

Published immediately after Terence MacSwiney, Lord Mayor of Cork, died in Brixton prison on hunger strike, this cartoon shows the Prime Minister, David Lloyd George, being confronted with the tragedy of MacSwiney's death by a veiled female figure—presumably a representation of Ireland in mourning. Lloyd George is contemptuously dismissed as a 'little man', dwarfed by MacSwiney in the latter's moment of self-sacrifice.

The Figure—'Hush, little man. You know how to live, but my concern is with one greater than thou—one who knows how to die.'

4. 'The Carson Kids'
Freeman's Journal, 18 November 1920

HERE IS A FINE EXAMPLE of how Shemus suggests a particular angle on events by placing his subjects in comical situations. It is one of only three Shemus cartoons in the National Library's archive to have been finished in watercolour. Lloyd George and Sir Hamar Greenwood are portrayed as children clutching Sir Edward Carson's apron strings. The implication is that, with Lloyd George dependent on the support of the Conservative Party to continue in office, Carson can dictate British policy in Ireland. In its main editorial published on the same day, the *Freeman* noted that 'reprisals still continue' and asked: 'Will [Mr Lloyd George] call off his dogs of war, or will he cry "Havoc!" and whoop them at the bidding of Sir Edward Carson?'

Hamar [in pin-stripes]—'Don't let go, Davy.'
Davy—'If I did I'd be lost, wouldn't I, Hamar?'

5. 'Awaiting the Note'*

Freeman's Journal, 14 July 1921

* Shemus suggested 'The Dawn' as the title of this cartoon.

THE THEME OF THIS CARTOON, which appeared in the *Freeman* just a few days after the Truce was declared in July 1921, is that Ireland is poised to achieve her freedom after 'many a year'. The iconic figure of Erin will then play her harp again. In the cartoon, Erin is looking eastwards. Lloyd George and de Valera were due to meet—and did meet—for the first time for settlement talks in London on the day the cartoon was published. It uses a more traditional image than is normally found in Shemus' work, harking back to the style of cartoons published in the *Freeman* and other organs of Irish nationalist opinion in the late 19th century. The published title is subtly less optimistic in tone than the one suggested by Shemus.

''Tis many a year since the strings sounded a song of hope and gladness, but the melody has not died in my heart.'

Young Ireland—'Why are you weeping, mother? The soldiers are going.'
Ireland—'That cannot be true, my child. They are not marching away. And who is keeping them here? Why am I still in bondage, and why are my children in prison?'

6. 'Why?'

Freeman's Journal, 23 December 1921.

The *Freeman*'s contempt for those opposed to the Anglo-Irish Treaty signed on 6 December 1921 is captured in this cartoon. The anti-Treatyites have been blocking the ratification of the Treaty by Dáil Éireann, thus denying Ireland the freedom that it would confer. As in fig. 5, Ireland is represented as a female figure. She is disconsolate and bound in chains. She doubts the assurance given to her by 'Young Ireland'—a boy embodying the future of the country—that 'the soldiers are going' and questions why she is 'still in bondage'. The reason is, of course, the failure of the Dáil to ratify the Treaty. In its main editorial on the same day, the *Freeman* stated that 'Dáil Éireann has adjourned its debate on the Treaty until January 3rd. So Ireland must pass its Christmas still under the shadow.' The building in the background is the Bank of Ireland in College Green, Dublin, the seat of the last Irish parliament before the Act of Union of 1800. This evokes the *Freeman*'s famous emblem—a sunburst behind the old parliament building—adopted in 1891 as an expression of the newspaper's Home Rule aspirations.[1]

1. The emblem was incorporated in the headpiece over the *Freeman*'s main editorials. The headpiece for 1 July 1922 is shown on the first page of this book.

7. 'Giving Him His Lines'*

Freeman's Journal, 10 February 1922

* Shemus suggested 'The Autocrats' as the title of this cartoon, and proposed a simpler caption as follows:
Childers—'Come now, that's something like a get-up.'

De Valera is depicted here as the mouthpiece of Erskine Childers. Childers was—to quote F. S. L. Lyons— 'intellectually one of the most formidable opponents of the Treaty',[1] and there was particular animosity towards him in the pro-Treaty camp. Arthur Griffith attacked him in Dáil Éireann at the end of the Treaty debate as a 'damned Englishman', and Piaras Béaslaí later wrote of him as 'this English ex-officer, who had spent his life in the service of England and English Imperialism'.[2] The *Freeman* faithfully reflected that animosity, and boosted it. An editorial published on the same day as the cartoon warned that de Valera was 'in danger . . . from the Childers' medicine', a message reinforced in the cartoon by attributing Childers' influence over de Valera to flattery. A later cartoon ('If Winter Comes', published on 13 May 1922) claimed that opposition to the Treaty would bring famine and other disasters to Ireland, and blamed Childers for inspiring that opposition. Childers was executed by firing squad in Beggars Bush Barracks on 24 November 1922, having been found guilty by a military tribunal of the unauthorised possession of a gun. It was, in fact, a 'little souvenir revolver' that Michael Collins had given him.[3] The *Freeman* re-used de Valera's head from this cartoon in an editorial highly critical of him on 28 December 1922—an extraordinary departure from normal practice: this was the only time an illustration was ever included in a *Freeman* editorial.

1 F. S. L. Lyons, *Ireland since the Famine* (London, 1971), p. 443.
2 Piaras Béaslaí, *Michael Collins and the making of a new Ireland*, 2 vols (London, 1926), ii, p. 354.
3 Andrew Boyle, *The Riddle of Erskine Childers* (London, 1977), p. 319.

Childers [from back]— 'That's fine. They fit you as well as ever—all except the cap, but that can't be helped. Now, don't forget to say it exactly as I told you.'

8. 'For Ireland's Sake'

Freeman's Journal, 12 April 1922

A MONUMENTAL FIGURE of Erin stands before representatives of the two sides in the Treaty controversy—the 'regular' pro-Treaty soldier on the left, the 'irregular' anti-Treaty gunman on the right—and pleads for peace.[1] This cartoon is a powerful and even-handed response to the announcement of a peace conference arranged by the Roman Catholic Archbishop of Dublin and the Lord Mayor of Dublin to try to resolve the differences between the pro- and anti-Treatyites and halt the drift towards civil war in Ireland. The talks—which took place soon afterwards in Dublin's Mansion House—were unsuccessful.

1 'Monumental' is one of the five categories of representations of Erin in late Victorian cartoons identified by Professor Curtis in *Images of Erin* (see note 23 on p. 23 above).

Erin—'Peace, my sons, for my sake.'

9. 'It Means Nothing to Them'*
Freeman's Journal, 26 April 1922

* Shemus suggested 'No Uncertain Voice' as the title of this cartoon, and proposed a slightly different caption as follows:
1st Militarist—'What's that deafening noise?'
2nd Militarist—'That's the voice of the people.'

Published shortly after the occupation of the Four Courts in Dublin by armed anti-Treatyites—the prelude to the outbreak of the Civil War—this cartoon has an unambiguous message. It is that armed resistance to the Treaty, symbolised by the skilfully drawn gunmen in the foreground, flouts majority opinion in Ireland. The building in the background is the Bank of Ireland in College Green, Dublin, the seat of the last Irish parliament before the Act of Union of 1800—see fig. 6. On the day the cartoon was published, the *Freeman* also carried a photograph of anti-Treaty forces arranging sandbags at the Four Courts under the headline 'Mutineers Prepare for a Siege'.

1st Militarist—'What's all the noise?'
2nd Militarist—'Don't worry. It's only the voice of the unarmed people.'

10. 'The Hold-Up'*

Freeman's Journal, 28 April 1922

* Shemus proposed 'The Wreckers' as the title of this cartoon.

SUGGESTING THAT THE anti-Treatyites—in particular, those who resort to armed force—are sabotaging the freedom that the Treaty has secured for Ireland, this cartoon echoes the *Freeman*'s main editorial on the same day. This proclaimed: 'The Irish Treaty represents gain, not loss; a victory, not defeat. But the people are to be denied freedom and peace without consultation because it does not contain something more which may readily come by the process of political evolution.' This is a classic statement of the case against the anti-Treatyites, a case vindicated by subsequent events. The cartoon is different from most other Shemus cartoons in that there is no caption, and none is required.

FREEDOM
SHEMUS.

DANIEL O'CONNELL
OWEN ROE O'NEILL
PARNELL
ARTHUR GRIFFITH
MICHAEL COLLINS.
DAVIS
ROBERT EMMETT
TONE
SHEMUS

11. 'Ireland's Via Dolorosa'
Freeman's Journal, 24 August 1922

MICHAEL COLLINS was shot dead at Béal na Bláth, Co. Cork on 22 August 1922 and this cartoon shows a female figure representing Ireland prostrate with grief at his death. The broken column is a traditional symbol for a life cut short, and each column in the cartoon bears the name of an Irish leader whose work was thwarted by untimely death. Collins is the latest in a line that includes Arthur Griffith, John Redmond, Charles Stewart Parnell, Daniel O'Connell, Robert Emmet, Wolfe Tone and Owen Roe O'Neill.[1] The broken columns mark out Ireland's 'Via Dolorosa', or 'Way of Sorrows'. Again, there is no caption—as in fig. 10. A slightly different version of this cartoon was published on 28 August 1922, the day of Collins' funeral in Dublin, under the title 'Ireland's Tribute'.

1 The monument marking the grave of Arthur Griffith in Glasnevin cemetery in Dublin actually takes the form of a broken column—'unfinished like his work, broken like his will' (Anne Dolan, *Commemorating the Irish Civil War: history and memory, 1923–2000* (Cambridge, 2003), p. 120).

12. 'Under the Greenwood Tree'*
Freeman's Journal, 30 April 1921

* Shemus' suggestion as a caption for this cartoon was the following:
Lloyd George—'We've got at the truth at last!'
And the Greenwood tree shook itself with laughter.

THE *FREEMAN'S* SENSE of its own role in the unfolding events in Ireland is represented here. Its fearless reporting is frustrating the efforts of Lloyd George and Sir Hamar Greenwood to cover up the truth about British policy. The title of the cartoon links Greenwood's surname with an easily recognisable passage from Shakespeare's *As You Like It* : "Under the greenwood tree,/Who loves to lie with me".[1] Greenwood is thus depicted as a tree against which Lloyd George lies, his left foot holding down a copy of the *Freeman*—and perhaps 'lies' has a double meaning here. On the day the cartoon was published, the *Freeman* reported that its premises had been raided by crown forces twice during the previous evening and some correspondence removed. The cartoon was a response to this unwelcome intrusion, though the *Freeman* had not been singled out by the crown forces; there had been a shooting incident nearby, and other offices in the area were also raided.

1 *As You Like It* (1599), act 2, sc. 1.

The Spirit of the Wood—'Keep your foot on it, David.'
Lloyd George—'But it's not comfortable. I get pins and needles.'

13. Untitled
Freeman's Journal, 22 April 1922

CELEBRATING THE *FREEMAN*'S re-launch less than a month after the destruction of its printing presses by a raiding party of anti-Treatyites on 29 March 1922, this cartoon shows a phoenix rising from the ashes of the wrecked *Freeman* plant, holding a copy of the newspaper in its beak. The cartoon was published in the first issue of the *Freeman* when it resumed normal production after its plant was replaced. While normal publication was suspended, a much reduced version of the *Freeman* was produced on Gestetner machines. A copy of the *Freeman* in its reduced form can be seen in the top right-hand corner. There is no caption—the cartoon is self-explanatory.

The Freeman's Journal
SUPPRESSED AGAIN!
SHEMUS

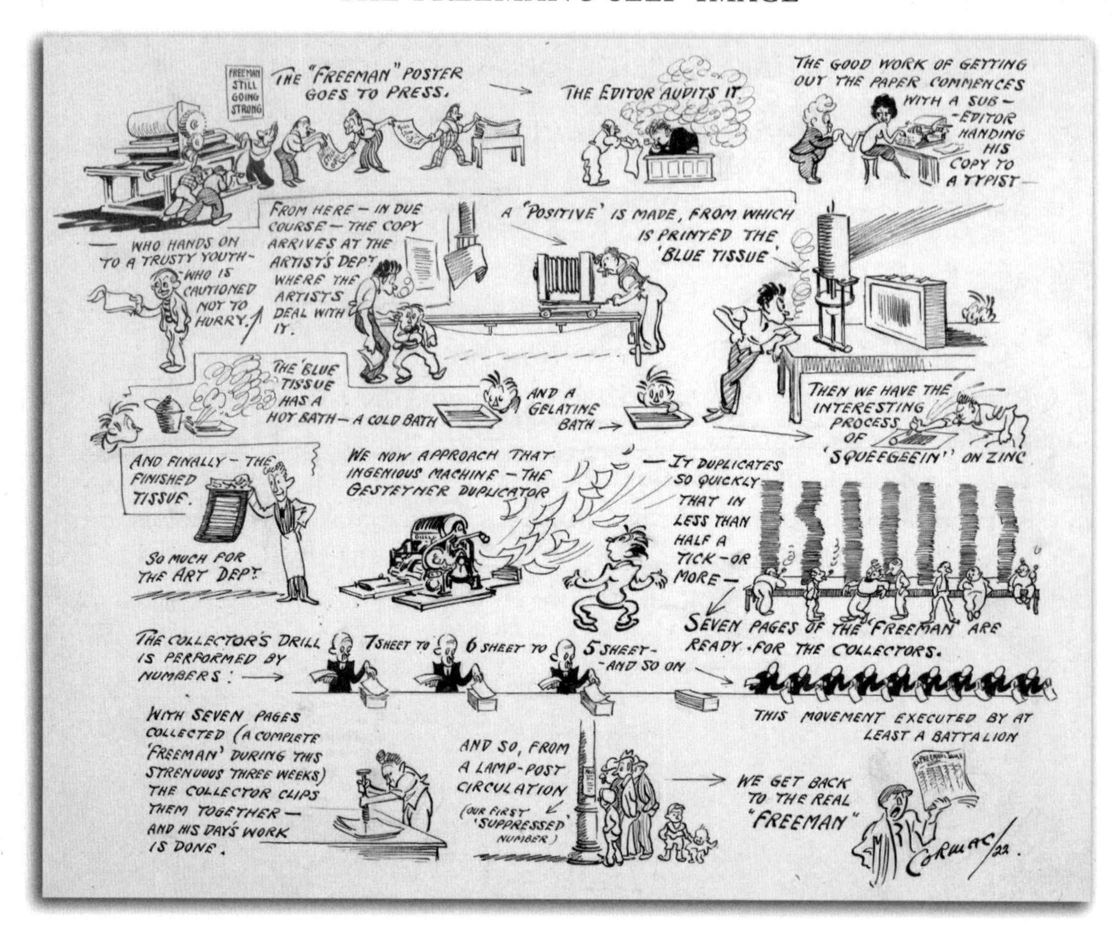
FREEMAN STILL GOING STRONG
THE "FREEMAN" POSTER GOES TO PRESS.
THE EDITOR AUDITS IT.
THE GOOD WORK OF GETTING OUT THE PAPER COMMENCES WITH A SUB-EDITOR HANDING HIS COPY TO A TYPIST —
— WHO HANDS ON TO A TRUSTY YOUTH — WHO IS CAUTIONED NOT TO HURRY.
FROM HERE — IN DUE COURSE — THE COPY ARRIVES AT THE ARTIST'S DEPT. WHERE THE ARTISTS DEAL WITH IT.
A 'POSITIVE' IS MADE, FROM WHICH IS PRINTED THE 'BLUE TISSUE'
THE 'BLUE TISSUE' HAS A HOT BATH — A COLD BATH
AND A GELATINE BATH
THEN WE HAVE THE INTERESTING PROCESS OF 'SQUEEGEEIN'' ON ZINC
AND FINALLY — THE FINISHED TISSUE.
SO MUCH FOR THE ART DEPT.
WE NOW APPROACH THAT INGENIOUS MACHINE — THE GESTETNER DUPLICATOR
— IT DUPLICATES SO QUICKLY THAT IN LESS THAN HALF A TICK — OR MORE —
SEVEN PAGES OF THE 'FREEMAN' ARE READY FOR THE COLLECTORS.
THE COLLECTOR'S DRILL IS PERFORMED BY NUMBERS:
7 SHEET TO 6 SHEET TO 5 SHEET — AND SO ON
THIS MOVEMENT EXECUTED BY AT LEAST A BATTALION
WITH SEVEN PAGES COLLECTED (A COMPLETE 'FREEMAN' DURING THIS STRENUOUS THREE WEEKS) THE COLLECTOR CLIPS THEM TOGETHER — AND HIS DAY'S WORK IS DONE.
AND SO, FROM A LAMP-POST CIRCULATION
(OUR FIRST 'SUPPRESSED' NUMBER)
WE GET BACK TO THE REAL "FREEMAN"
CORMAC/22.

14. 'Cormac's Vision of the Interregnum'*
Freeman's Journal, 22 April 1922

* The title Forbes suggested for this cartoon was 'How we made a little *Freeman*'.

A MUCH REDUCED VERSION of the *Freeman* was produced on Gestetner machines as a stop-gap following the destruction of the newspaper's printing plant by a raiding party of anti-Treatyites on 29 March 1922. This cartoon shows the process involved. It appeared in a supplement published with the first issue of the *Freeman* when it resumed normal production. The cartoon is signed 'Cormac', a pseudonym that Forbes usually used for cartoons about sporting events. It is in the same style and has the same layout as the other Cormac cartoons.

Colonel Moore.
Ernest Forbes.

15. 'Snapped by Shemus' portrait no. 8—Senator Colonel Maurice Moore *Freeman's Journal*, 1 March 1923

MAURICE MOORE (1854–1939), a scion of the Catholic gentry of Connacht, was a member of the Senate of the Irish Free State for the entire period of its existence (1922–36). His ancestral home—Moore Hall, overlooking Lough Carra, in Co. Mayo—was burned down by the anti-Treatyites in February 1923. His brother George was the author of *Hail and Farewell* and numerous other works. Maurice had a distinguished military career with the Connaught Rangers, being promoted Colonel while serving in South Africa during the Boer War. After 1913, he helped to organise the Irish Volunteers—though, as noted by Professor F. X. Martin, 'representing the opposite end . . . of the political scale within the Volunteers' from P. H. Pearse.[1] He joined Fianna Fáil in 1928. In 1931 he was defeated in an election for vice-chairman of the Senate by Senator Patrick J. Hooper. Hooper had been the last editor of the *Freeman's Journal* from 1916 to 1924.[2] This caricature is signed Ernest Forbes rather than Shemus.

1 F. X. Martin, 'MacNeill and the foundation of the Irish Volunteers' in F .X. Martin and F. J. Byrne (eds), *The scholar revolutionary: Eoin MacNeill, 1897–1945, and the making of the new Ireland* (Dublin, 1973), p. 137, n.53.

2 I have written the entry on Patrick J. Hooper for the Royal Irish Academy's *Dictionary of Irish Biography* (Cambridge, 2009).

16. 'Snapped by Shemus' portrait no. 16—George Gavan Duffy TD
Freeman's Journal, 12 March 1923

GEORGE GAVAN DUFFY (1882–1951) was the son of Sir Charles Gavan Duffy, the Young Irelander. Born in Cheshire, he had practised as a solicitor in London and represented Sir Roger Casement there after the Easter Rising in 1916. He then came to Ireland and was called to the Irish Bar in 1917. Elected to the first, second and third Dáil, he was a member of the Irish delegation that signed the Anglo-Irish Treaty in 1921. Afterwards, he briefly served as Minister for Foreign Affairs in 1922. He unsuccessfully contested the 1923 general election as an independent candidate. In 1936 he was appointed a High Court judge, and was promoted to President of the High Court in 1946. A staunch defender of individual rights against the State, he is regarded by many authorities as the father of judicial review in Ireland.[1] See also fig. 25.

1 See Louis McRedmond (ed.), *Modern Irish lives: dictionary of 20th century biography* (Dublin 1996), p. 89.

Gavin Duffy
SHEMUS

17. 'Snapped by Shemus' portrait no. 39— General Richard Mulcahy *Freeman's Journal*, 13 April 1923

RICHARD MULCAHY (1886–1971) was chief of staff of the IRA during the War of Independence and succeeded Michael Collins as commander-in-chief of the Irish army. He was Minister for Defence in the government of the Free State from 1922 until 1924, when he resigned after being criticised by a government-appointed inquiry for his handling of the recent 'Army Mutiny'. He later served as Minister for Local Government and Public Health (1927–32) and as Minister for Education (1948–51, 1954–7). Leader of the Fine Gael Party from 1944 to 1959, he was a TD almost continuously from 1918 to 1961.

General Mulcahy
SHEMUS

18. 'Snapped by Shemus' portrait no. 43—Ernest Blythe

Freeman's Journal, 18 April 1923

Ernest Blythe (1889–1975) was Minister for Local Government from 1922 to September 1923. He then became Minister for Finance, a portfolio he held until 1932. He succeeded Kevin O'Higgins as Vice-President of the Executive Council of the Free State in 1927. As Minister for Finance, he had to bear the brunt of the criticism of the decision to cut old age pensions by a shilling and reduce the pay of teachers and the police to cope with the depression of the early 1930s. He lost his Dáil seat in 1933, but was a member of the Free State Senate from 1934 until its abolition in 1936. He was afterwards managing director of the Abbey Theatre (1939–67). Note the double signature on this caricature—Shemus and Ernest Forbes.

SHEMUS.
Ernest Forbes.

19. 'Snapped by Shemus' portrait no. 58—Stanley Baldwin

Freeman's Journal, 24 May 1923

When this portrait appeared, Stanley Baldwin (1867–1947) had just become British Prime Minister for the first time. He had been a relatively obscure figure in the Conservative Party until his appointment as Chancellor of the Exchequer in October 1922, and so was a surprise choice as Prime Minister. In its main editorial on the previous day (23 May 1923), the *Freeman* said of him that 'there is no record of measures to his name, and all we know of his principles is that his complacency towards the Die-hards [the extreme Conservatives in the House of Commons] has hoisted him to the highest office in record time'. A 'die-hard' archetype is accordingly shown standing behind Baldwin in the portrait. Baldwin served as Prime Minister for three separate periods (May 1923–January 1924, November 1924–1929, 1935–1937). He was Prime Minister during the General Strike of 1926 and the abdication crisis of 1936.

England's new
Prime Minister.
SHEMUS

20. 'The Six Counties' (no caption)
Freeman's Journal, 28 May 1921

THIS CARTOON MARKS the introduction of partition under the Government of Ireland Act 1920. The first elections to the new parliament of Northern Ireland had just taken place. In the cartoon, the six counties of Northern Ireland are symbolised by bubbles blown from Sir Edward Carson's toy pipe. Sir James Craig, the first Prime Minister of Northern Ireland, is borne aloft on top of the bubbles, while Lloyd George and Sir Hamar Greenwood look on from a distance. There is no caption, as in figs. 10, 11, 13 and 14 above—unusual for a Shemus cartoon.

SHEMUS.

21. 'Henry, The Ruthless'*
Freeman's Journal, 8 June 1922

* Shemus suggested 'Tactics' as the title of this cartoon, and proposed the following caption:
His Orderly—'All is quiet in the salient, sir!'
Field Marshal Wilson—'But there's a hell of a row everywhere else'.

SIR HENRY WILSON, a native of Co. Longford and former Chief of the Imperial General Staff in London (see fig. 2), became Unionist MP for North Down at Westminster in February 1922, and in March 1922 was appointed advisor on security matters to the new government of Northern Ireland. He was perceived as strongly anti-nationalist, and the *Freeman* held him responsible for the spate of sectarian violence directed against the Catholic population of Belfast. In the cartoon, the Grim Reaper reports back to Wilson—thereby signalling where responsibility lies for 'the Belfast orgy of sabotage and slaughter' (to quote from the *Freeman*'s main editorial on 30 May 1922). It is a troubling image in view of the fact that Wilson was himself shot dead by two IRA men in London just a fortnight after the cartoon was published. Keith Jeffery's recent biography of Wilson demonstrates that he was, in fact, a relatively moderate voice within Ulster unionist circles.[1] The *Freeman*'s campaign against him had a curious symmetry with its campaign against Erskine Childers (see fig. 7)—in both cases the *Freeman* was guilty of encouraging widely held prejudices, which led to their deaths.

1 Keith Jeffery, *Field-Marshal Sir Henry Wilson: a political soldier* (Oxford, 2006), pp 279–80.

The Grim Reaper—'All correct, sir?'

Surgeon McGuffin [on right]—'This Boundary Question is swollen out of all proportion.'
Craig—'It gives me a pain every time I stop to examine it.'

22. 'Appendicitis' (n.d.)

THIS CARTOON IS CRITICAL of Sir James Craig and the Northern Ireland government for their reluctance to engage in discussions about adjustments to the boundary between Northern Ireland and the Free State. The Anglo-Irish Treaty of 1921 had provided for such adjustments 'in accordance with the wishes of the inhabitants', with a Boundary Commission to determine the adjustments. It was assumed by both sides that some of the territory of Northern Ireland would be transferred to the Free State. The Boundary Commission was eventually appointed in 1924, but the Northern Ireland government refused to co-operate with it. It never formally reported, and the boundary was not altered—precisely the outcome that the Ulster unionists wanted.[1] Craig is shown with Samuel McGuffin, a hard-line unionist member of the Northern Ireland parliament and leader of the Ulster Unionist Labour Association. It has not been possible to confirm when—or even whether—this cartoon was published in the *Freeman*, though it is part of the archive of Shemus cartoons acquired by the National Library in 2006. Given its subject, it is likely to date from December 1922 when the boundary question was discussed in the Northern Ireland parliament—with contributions to the debate from both Craig and McGuffin.[2]

1 For further information on the Boundary Commission, see Geoffrey J. Hand, 'MacNeill and the Boundary Commission' in Martin and Byrne (eds), *The scholar revolutionary: Eoin MacNeill, 1897-1945, and the making of the new Ireland* (Dublin, 1973), pp 199–275.
2 The debate was reported in the *Freeman* on 8 December 1922.

23. 'Drawn to Scale'
Freeman's Journal, 2 October 1923

THIS CARTOON ATTACKS the gerrymandering of local government constituencies by the Northern Ireland government—without 'consideration for democratic principles or fair play' (to quote from an editorial in the *Freeman* on 26 September 1923). That editorial gave an example of gerrymandering from the Omagh rural district council in Co. Tyrone: 'whereas a Unionist can be elected with 228 votes, a Nationalist will require 463, or more than double'. In other words, 'it takes two Nationalists to make a Unionist'. The cartoon conveys the injustice of this is by juxtaposing two puny Nationalists against the bulky form of Sir James Craig, who is ridiculed as the Belfast Colossus. Both this cartoon and the preceding one (fig. 22) are good examples of Shemus' skill in exaggerating an unflattering characteristic of an individual—in these instances, Sir James Craig's bulk—for the purpose of making a political point. Unusually, this cartoon is not signed.

1st Nationalist—'According to the new vote distribution in Ulster, it takes two Nationalists to make a Unionist!'
2nd Nationalist (his eye on the Belfast Colossus)—'I admit it.'

24. 'Ulster Will Fight, Etc.'
Freeman's Journal, 29 June 1923

MANY SOUTHERN IRISH UNIONISTS, feeling abandoned as an insignificant minority in the Free State emigrated to England.[1] Here a group of them confronts Sir Edward Carson, now Lord Carson of Duncairn, with the failure of his strategy of using Ulster—in other words, playing 'the Orange card'—to preserve the union between Britain and the entire island of Ireland. He, on the other hand, expresses his disillusionment with England for its betrayal of the Southern Irish unionists. He was himself a Southern Irish unionist, and his personal sense of betrayal was evident in his speech to the House of Lords in December 1921 on the Anglo-Irish Treaty, in which he famously declared: 'What a fool I was. I was only a puppet, and so was Ulster, and so was Ireland, in the political game that was to get the Conservative Party into power. And of all the men in my experience that I think are the most loathsome, it is those who will sell their friends for the purpose of conciliating their enemies.'[2]

1 But see Ian d'Alton, 'Remembering the future, imagining the past: how southern Irish Protestants survived' in Felix M. Larkin (ed.), *Librarians, poets and scholars: a Festschrift for Dónall Ó Luanaigh* (Dublin, 2007), pp 212–30, especially pp 227–9.
2 Quoted in Geoffrey Lewis, *Carson: the man who divided Ireland* (London, 2005), p. 231.

Carson [on right] to Southern Unionist Exiles—'I'm sorry I ever told you to trust England!'
Southern Unionist Chorus—'We're sorry you ever told us to trust Ulster!'

25. 'Internment'
Freeman's Journal, 14 July 1923

THIS CARTOON PRESENTS a panorama of the chamber during the first ever all-night sitting of Dáil Éireann. In adjacent news columns, the *Freeman* reported that the Dáil had adjourned at 8 a.m. the previous day after a seventeen-hour debate and that 'at five o'clock yesterday morning a small number of deputies were sound asleep on the benches, but the debate went on with no sign of slackening'. The matter under debate was a Public Safety Bill to permit *inter alia* the continued detention of anti-Treaty prisoners without trial, and the title of the cartoon implies that the deputies had likewise been imprisoned in the Dáil chamber in order to pass this measure into law. The opposition to the measure was led by George Gavan Duffy, the bearded figure shown addressing the Dáil in the cartoon. The entry on Gavan Duffy in the *Oxford DNB* describes him as 'an unswerving advocate of human rights and the rule of law',[1] and he had resigned from the government in 1922 in protest against the increasingly arbitrary nature of the government's treatment of anti-Treaty prisoners. A portrait of him in the 'Snapped by Shemus' series had appeared in the *Freeman* on 12 March 1923 (fig. 16). Other figures in the cartoon include William T. Cosgrave (President of the Executive Council), Patrick Hogan (Minister for Agriculture) and Desmond FitzGerald (Minister for Foreign Affairs)—all three seated on the government front bench, on the left-hand side. The Ceann Comhairle (or Speaker) of the Dáil, Professor Michael Hayes, is seen from behind in the foreground.

1 H. C. G. Matthew and Brian Harrison (eds), *Oxford Dictionary of National Biography*, 60 vols (Oxford, 2004), xvii, pp 142–3.

The Dáil rose at 8 a.m. on Friday after an all-night sitting.

Appendix
'Snapped by Shemus': list of subjects, in alphabetical order, with dates of publication

*Stanley Baldwin MP: May 24, 1923
Senator William Barrington: June 27, 1923
Richard Beamish: March 3, 1923
*Senator T. W. Westropp Bennett: March 19, 1923
Sarah Bernhardt: March 28, 1923
*Ernest Blythe: TD: April 18, 1923
Sir Edward Carson: March 2, 1923
Lord Robert Cecil: May 26, 1923
Walter L. Cole TD: July 19, 1923
*Ald. Richard Corish TD: May 18, 1923
W. T. Cosgrave TD: March 5, 1923
Senator John J. Counihan: May 11, 1923
Sir James Craig MP: March 9, 1923
Sir James Craig TD: May 25, 1923
*William Davin TD: April 6, 1923
*Robert Day TD: June 1, 1923
Joseph Devlin MP: April 28, 1923
Steve Donoghue: March 22, 1923
*Senator James G. Douglas: April 9, 1923
Lynn Doyle: March 14, 1923
*George Gavan Duffy TD: March 12, 1923
*E. J. Duggan TD: March 15, 1923
Senator Sir Thomas Grattan Esmonde, Bart: March 24, 1923
*James Everett TD: June 23, 1923
Senator E. W. Eyre: March 27, 1923
*Darrell Figgis TD: February 20, 1923
*Desmond FitzGerald TD: March 13, 1923
Gerald Fitzgibbon TD: June 2, 1923
Sir Joseph Glynn: June 22, 1923
Senator Oliver St John Gogarty: March 16, 1923
The Earl of Granard: May 12, 1923
*Senator Sir John Purser Griffiths: April 2, 1923
Senator Henry Seymour Guinness: April 14, 1923
Senator Benjamin Haughton: May 15, 1923
*Senator The Marquess of Headford: March 23, 1923
Paul Henry: June 16, 1923
Professor R. M. Henry: July 3, 1923
P. J. Hogan TD: May 8, 1923
*Senator Cornelius J. Irwin: April 4, 1923
Senator Andrew Jameson: April 16, 1923
Thomas Johnson TD: February 24, 1923
*Senator Sir John Keane, Bart: April 20, 1923
Hugh Kennedy KC: February 21, 1923
Senator P. W. Kenny: March 26, 1923
*Senator The Earl of Kerry: April 17, 1923

* Denotes original drawing(s) in the National Library collection.

Sir John Lavery: May 5, 1923
Senator Thomas Linehan: April 21, 1923
Sir Thomas Lipton: March 10, 1923
Lord Londonderry: April 10, 1923
*Senator Joseph Clayton Love: April 3, 1923
Reginald McKenna MP: May 29, 1923
*Senator John MacLoughlin: April 23, 1923
Senator Edward MacLysaght: March 31, 1923
Eoin MacNeill: May 22, 1923
Lord Monteagle: February 23, 1923
*Senator Col. Maurice Moore: March 1, 1923
*Senator James Moran: April 5, 1923
*General Richard Mulcahy: April 13, 1923
*Ald. William O'Brien TD: April 12, 1923
Daniel O'Callaghan TD: April 27, 1923
T. J. O'Connell TD: June 26, 1923
Kevin O'Higgins TD: April 7, 1923
Sir William Orpen: February 27, 1923
Cathal O'Shannon TD: March 7, 1923
Senator Hutcheson Poë, Bart: May 30, 1923
*Capt. William Redmond: March 8, 1923
William Sears: May 19, 1923
George Bernard Shaw: February 19, 1923
Davy Stephens: June 6, 1923
Daniel Vaughan TD: June 30, 1923
Professor Joseph Whelehan TD: July 6, 1923
The Earl of Wicklow: March 17, 1923
Jack B. Yeats: May 2, 1923
William Butler Yeats: February 26, 1923

The title page of *The reign of terror* (1922), a selection of Shemus' cartoons originally published in the *Freeman* between April 1920 and June 1921. The publication is discussed on p. 21 above.

Index of names